# Mental Maths
## for ages 7 to 9

## Teacher's book

## Anita Straker

**CAMBRIDGE**
UNIVERSITY PRESS

For Ella, who is just learning to count.

PUBLISHED BY THE PRESS SYNDICATE OF THE UNIVERSITY OF CAMBRIDGE
The Pitt Building, Trumpington Street, Cambridge CB2 1RP, United Kingdom

CAMBRIDGE UNIVERSITY PRESS
The Edinburgh Building, Cambridge CB2 2RU, United Kingdom
40 West 20th Street, New York, NY10011-4211, USA
10 Stamford Road, Oakleigh, Melbourne 3166, Australia

© Cambridge University Press 1994

First published 1994
Fourth printing 1998

Printed in the United Kingdom at the University Press, Cambridge

A catalogue record for this book is available from the British Library.

ISBN 0 521 48509 6

# Introduction

This series is intended to help children think about numbers and carry out mental calculations. There are three teacher's books and seven booklets of short exercises for pupils: one teacher's book and one booklet for children aged 5 to 7, a second teacher's book and two more booklets for ages 7 to 9, and a third teacher's book and three more booklets for ages 9 to 11. The final pupil's booklet is mainly for lower secondary pupils.

*Mental Maths for ages 7 to 9* is the second teacher's book. It contains ideas for you to work on with groups of children or a whole class and photocopiable pages of puzzles and games for children to do by themselves. *Mental Maths 1* and *Mental Maths 2* are published separately and are intended for seven- to nine-year-olds to work from directly, either at school or at home.

## Part 1: Ways of working                                        Page 2
Part 1 of this book contains brief advice on things like classroom organisation and ways in which children can record their answers. It stresses the importance of counting activities and the value of discussing children's methods.

## Part 2: Oral work                                              Page 7
Part 2 has a series of suggestions for oral work at national curriculum levels 2 to 4. Each activity is designed to be led by a teacher or classroom assistant and will last for up to 10 minutes. The level of difficulty and the number skills required are indicated for each one. Many of the activities are suitable for a whole class to work on together, since questions and responses are possible at more than one level. Others are more suitable for a small group working at roughly the same level.

## Part 3: Puzzles and games                                      Page 27
Part 3 consists of photocopiable pages of puzzles or games for children to work on by themselves. The puzzles are for individual children to do, either in school or at home. The games are intended for two or more children to play together. Most children will be able to read the instructions or the rules for themselves though less confident readers may need some help. In most cases, children will be able to complete the activity in about 15 minutes. Levels of difficulty for each activity, and solutions to the puzzles, are given on pages 60 to 62.

## Answers: *Mental Maths 1 & 2*                                  Page 63
*Mental Maths 1*, the first of the two children's booklets for ages 7 to 9, contains exercises at levels 2 or 3 of the national curriculum; *Mental Maths 2* focuses mainly on level 3 and touches on level 4. The intention is that children should work regularly on just one or two of the 5- to 10-minute exercises or problems each week throughout the course of the two years. Answers to the questions in the two booklets are given at the back of this book on pages 63 to 70. They are also in the *Answer Book* which accompanies the whole series.

# Part 1: Ways of working

## Mental work with numbers

The importance of mental arithmetic and the ability to think about numbers in one's head is undeniable. Although many jobs require an ability to calculate using tools like calculators or computers, in everyday life an ability to deal mentally with numbers – combined with the occasional use of the back of an envelope – is of more use.

Quick recall of number facts and confidence with mental calculations – both those where an accurate answer is required and those where an approximation is good enough – will develop only if children have frequent and varied opportunities to practise. Short sessions of five minutes on most days are preferable to half-an-hour once a week. These can be fitted at the start or end of a day, or between two other activities, or at any time when the context provides an opportunity to talk about numbers. You could also use your sessions of thinking about numbers to:

- ❐ revise last week's number work;
- ❐ ask questions related to classroom displays;
- ❐ help children to use and apply mathematics to investigate or solve problems;
- ❐ extend their mathematical vocabulary;
- ❐ assess the skills of individual children.

## Organising the class

To achieve an atmosphere for thinking, you will need to establish the way that you want to work with the children. For example, you might say:

- ❐ Today we are going to think about numbers. We won't be using pencil and paper or calculators to help work things out – we will just use our heads.
- ❐ If you have something to say, or are ready to tell me your answer, don't call out as it might distract others who are still thinking.
- ❐ Try not to interrupt when anyone else is speaking.
- ❐ When you are thinking, it sometimes helps to shut your eyes.

When you are arranging groups of children to work together, you may need to consider the role that each could play. Pupils are more likely to learn if they take an active part but some may dominate and others may try to withdraw from the interaction. Your role is to ask questions, observe and give feedback, directing suitable questions to individuals and encouraging the more reluctant.

If a group is to be left to work on its own for a while, you may need to allocate particular responsibilities to different children. Some roles they can play are:

- a starter: who makes sure that everyone understands what is to be done and who calls you if the group gets stuck;
- an organiser: who collects whatever materials are needed for the activity, gives them out to everyone in the group, and gathers them together at the end;
- a reader: who helps anyone understand any difficult words;
- a time-keeper: who starts and stops the clock for any timed activities;
- a referee: who makes sure that turns are taken fairly and that everyone has an equal chance to contribute;
- a recorder: who has pencil and paper to note any scores;
- a reporter: who agrees with the group what will be reported to you or to the whole class at the end of the activity.

## Recording answers in oral work

Most of the answers to your questions will be given orally. This helps to build children's confidence and speed without the need for any formal recording.

However, with larger groups it is more difficult to involve everyone if all the answers are spoken. There are various strategies for recording which help to ensure that each child responds during mental arithmetic sessions.

- Answers up to 20 can be recorded on a number strip. Start each question by saying something like 'Colour this number blue.' At the end of your questions you can check their answers by asking 'Which number did you colour blue?' Children can also compare their patterns of colours to identify any errors.

- Another way is to give each member of the group a pack of number cards. Children simply pick from their packs the card which corresponds to their answer and put it in front of them on the table top or hold it up to show you.

- With two-digit answers, you can use sets of double width cards for numerals 10 to 90, and single width for 1 to 9. When you ask a question, each child places the appropriate units card on top of the tens card, and holds it on the table top while you check their responses. This also helps to reinforce place value.

$$\boxed{3\ 0} \quad \text{with} \quad \boxed{5} \quad \text{gives} \quad \boxed{3\,|\,5}$$

- Older pupils can, of course, write their answers on a piece of paper.

- An alternative is to provide them with a 100-square. As questions are asked, numbers corresponding to answers can be covered with a counter or coloured on the square. It is easy for you to walk round the class and see who has covered what.

**Responding to children's answers**

Praise is important, so how do you avoid discouragement when children give 'wrong' answers? Rather than saying 'yes' or 'no' to right or wrong answers, you can try saying:

❑ Has anyone got a different answer?
❑ What do other people think?
❑ Are there any other possibilities?

or

❑ How did you work that out?
❑ How could we check that?
❑ Did anyone do it a different way?

It is easier for children to come up with acceptable answers if occasionally you build in a longer thinking time for those who find it difficult. You could also ask children to agree an answer with a partner before going 'public'. More open-ended questions allow a wider range of possible answers and help to encourage the more diffident. For example:

❑ The answer is 4 cm. What was the question?
❑ Can you estimate the height of this room, or how much this bucket holds, or the number of words in this rhyme ...?
❑ I know that $20 \times 4$ is 80, so what else do I know?
   (For example, $10 \times 4 = 40, 20 \times 2 = 40, 200 \times 4 = 800, 20 \times 40 = 800$ ...)
❑ Approximately, what is $29 + 42$?

**Discussing the methods used**

Methods of mental arithmetic are based on a sound understanding of place value together with good recall of addition and multiplication facts. Your first aim is to build up children's speed and confidence in the recall of number facts, and to extend their awareness of the number system, without worrying about formal recording.

Next you need to help children develop their own strategies for mental calculations. Few people use the standard written methods when they are working in their heads. For example, it is not uncommon in mental calculations to add the hundreds or the tens first and then the units, or the pounds before the pence. You need to point this out and draw attention to the different ways of doing things. There is no 'proper' method – children can choose whatever method suits them best.

Every so often, you should ask children to explain their thinking to you and their class-mates. You could also explain to them your own ways of doing things, if these are different. The purpose of this is to help them to remember and refine the strategies they are using.

You could use questions like these to help children think about their methods.

- ❐ That's interesting. Could you tell us how you did it?
- ❐ I'm not sure I understand. Could you tell us more about that?
- ❐ Could you explain why you did it that way?
- ❐ When you began, did you think it would work out like that?

## The importance of counting

The ability to count with confidence in all kinds of situations underpins a lot of simple mental arithmetic. Almost any session can start with a quick counting activity. It is certainly worth checking at the start of the school year which children are confident with these lower level counting activities.

*Level 1*
- ❐ Say the number sequence *1, 2, 3* ... very slowly, very loudly, backwards, clapping as you say it ...
- ❐ Let's sing together 'One, two – three, four, five. Once I caught a fish alive ...' or 'Ten green bottles ...'
- ❐ Count these pebbles, buttons, straws ... You can touch them as you count.
- ❐ Count in your head till I say stop. What number did you reach? Now count aloud for me to that number.
- ❐ Count these cubes. They are all the same size and shape. Now count these bricks. They are different sizes and shapes.
- ❐ These counters are arranged neatly in a straight line. Can you count them? Count these. They are all over the place but you can move them as you count. Now count these. You can touch them if you want to, but don't move them. Now count these – but without touching them. How many are there?
- ❐ Count these spots – stuck on A4 cards – arranged in a straight line, in a regular pattern, all over the place.
- ❐ Count this tower of jumbo bricks. Now lay them in a long line on the floor. How many jumbo bricks now?
- ❐ Count some things you can't touch or reach: the window panes, the chairs in the room, the birds in the picture on the wall, the dogs on the 'pets' graph ...
- ❐ I'll say a number, and you count on – or back – from there.
- ❐ What number comes after 6? What number comes before 9? Two before 7?
- ❐ If we counted round the circle starting with Mary with 5, who would say 11? Think in your heads and tell me who it would be.
- ❐ Count these chime bar sounds to yourself, then tell me how many you heard – first at regular intervals, then irregular.
- ❐ Look at these cards with spots on (no more than 10, in identifiable groups such as twos and threes). Can you say how many spots there are without counting one by one? How did you know?
- ❐ Point to the fourth counter in this row. What colour is the seventh counter? Which counter is after the blue one? Point to the third red counter.

*Level 2*

❐ Let's count all our shoes in turn. Whisper your first number. Shout your second number. Which numbers did we whisper? Which did we shout?

❐ Say 'One two, buckle my shoe ...' or 'Two, four, six, eight. Mary at the garden gate ...'

❐ Count the even numbers. Count the odd numbers. Now count them backwards.

❐ Count in twos, starting with 6. Will we get to 37? How do you know?

❐ Take these 24 counters out of this bag and count them onto the table one at a time, two at a time, three at a time, four at a time.

❐ Look at these cards with spots on (no more than 20, randomly arranged, but in identifiable groups such as twos, threes or fours). Can you say how many spots there are without counting one by one? How did you know?

❐ Estimate how many spots there are on these cards when I hold them up briefly. Who thinks there are more than 15? Can you explain why?

❐ Count in tens to 100, and then back to nought.

❐ Now start at 5 and count in tens. Will you say 73? How do you know?

*Level 3*

❐ How many children in the class? How many legs, arms, eyes, fingers, toes ...?

❐ Count in twenties to 200. Now count backwards in twenties to zero.

❐ Count in hundreds to 1000 and back again.

❐ What number is the third before 31? What number is the fourth after 48?

❐ Count in threes to 30. Count in fours to 24.

❐ Start at 2 and count in threes. Start at 5 and count in fours.

❐ Start at 30 and count backwards in threes. Now start at 31.

❐ Start at 40 and count backwards in fours. Now start at 42.

❐ If everyone wore a cardigan with 5 buttons, how many buttons would there be altogether? How did you work it out?

❐ How many words do you think there are on this page of your reading book? What is a good way to estimate?

*Level 4*

❐ Choose any number. Count on – or back – in sixes, sevens, eights, nines.

❐ Count in twenty-fives to 1000. What is 75 more than 350? 50 less than 625?

❐ Play *Fizz Buzz* by counting round the class. For any multiple of 7 say *Fizz*. For any multiple of 6 say *Buzz*. If the number has both properties, say *Fizz Buzz*.

❐ Count on in sixes. What number should we stop at if, when we count back in sevens, we reach the same starting number? Why?

❐ This pattern of beads has three red, four blue, three red, four blue ... What colour is the 25th bead? What position is the 20th red bead?

## More hints

You will find more activities and advice about asking questions, prompting answers, developing vocabulary, and so on, in *Talking Points*, by Anita Straker, published by Cambridge University Press (ISBN 0 521 44758 5).

# Part 2: Oral work

These activities are intended to be led by you or by a classroom assistant. Some are suitable for the whole class and others for small groups. Most will take about ten minutes but some will need a little longer. In many of the activities no writing is needed, though children could record their answers in the ways described on page 3; in others, it is helpful to tabulate some of the results in order to look for patterns. An oral activity might be followed up by children working by themselves on a game or puzzle which draws on the same range of skills.

 ## Candy bars

### Objectives
Level 2:
addition of coins to 10p.

### Organisation
Work with a group of any size, or the whole class.

### Words to stress
Amount, sum, plus, total, value.

### Preparation
You will need a board or wall-chart on which to keep a record. Children might like some coins to experiment with at first, but encourage them to use their imaginations and to calculate mentally as much as possible.

### Procedure
Tell the children to imagine that they are buying a candy bar costing 5p from a slot machine. They have only 1p and 2p coins to pay with. Ask them:

❑ How could you pay for a candy bar costing 5p? Which coins would you use?
❑ Are there any other ways of paying this amount?
❑ Does the order of the coins matter? Does 2p + 2p + 1p have the same value as 2p + 1p + 2p?
❑ How many different ways can you make a total of 5p? *(Three ways: two 2p and one 1p, or one 2p and three 1p, or five 1p.)*
❑ What if the candy bar cost 6p? How many different ways of paying for it are there now? *(4)*
❑ What about cheaper bars costing 1p, 2p, 3p or 4p? How many different ways of paying for these are there? *(1, 2, 2, 3 respectively)*
❑ What about more expensive bars costing 7p, 8p, 9p, 10p? *(4, 5, 5, 6 respectively)*
❑ Could we record all our findings in a table?
❑ Can you predict how many different ways there are to pay for candy bars costing 11p or 12p? *(6, 7)*

# Domino sums

## Objectives
Level 2:
subtraction of 0 to 6
from 7, 8 or 9.

## Organisation
Work with a group of
about four children.
Children can continue to
play independently,
aiming for a different
total.

## Words to stress
Minus, subtract,
difference, how many
more?

## Preparation
You need a set of dominoes shuffled and divided face up
between the four children.

## Procedure
Choose a total of 8. On another day make the total 7 or 9.
The player with the double six places it on the table. The
next player puts down a domino making a total of 8 from
the touching spots. For example,

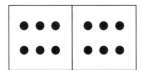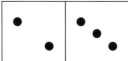

The next player now needs to find a domino with two
spots to go on the left, or with five spots to go on the right.
Play continues in turn until one player gets rid of all their
dominoes. If this is impossible, the player with the fewest
remaining dominoes wins the game. Prompt the children
with questions like:

❒ How many more are needed to make 8?
❒ What is the difference between 8 and 3?
❒ Subtract 3 from 8. What do you get?

# 3 Domino pairs

## Objectives
Level 2:
sum or difference of two
numbers from 0 to 6.

## Organisation
Work with a group of up
to four children.

## Words to stress
Add, plus, sum, total,
minus, difference.

## Preparation
Shuffle a set of dominoes and put them face down on a
table. Decide whether to make sums or differences.

## Procedure
Children take turns to turn over a domino and say the sum
or difference of the number of spots. If they can do so with
quick recall, they keep the domino. Otherwise it is put
back face down. Ask questions like these.

❒ What is the sum of (difference between) the spots?
❒ What is the total number? How many altogether?

**Flip-flop**

## Objectives
Level 2:
sum, difference, product or quotient of two numbers from 1 to 6.

## Organisation
Work with a group of any size, or the whole class.

## Words to stress
Plus, minus, multiply, divide, equals; sum, difference, product, quotient.

## Preparation
Each child should draw a grid like the one below. You also need two dice, which you or one of the group can roll.

| 0 | 1 | 2 | 3 | 4 |
|---|---|---|---|---|
| 5 | 6 | 7 | 8 | 9 |

## Procedure
Throw both dice. Children should try to make one of the numbers on their grid, writing their 'sum' (for example, $3 \times 3$) in the appropriate box. Emphasise that addition, subtraction, multiplication or division can be used. The first child to fill all their boxes calls out 'Flip-flop'. Ask:

❑ What would happen if you added or subtracted the numbers? What if you multiplied or divided them?
❑ What is the sum of the numbers? And the difference? What is the product? Or the quotient?

 **Estimates**

## Objectives
Level 2:
estimation and counting of a number up to 100; rounding of two-digit numbers.

## Organisation
Work with a small group.

## Words to stress
How many?
Guess, estimate, count, roughly, nearest.

## Preparation
Stick different numbers of shapes on A4 cards in random arrangements. You will also need up to 100 small cubes.

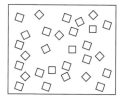

## Procedure
Ask each child to guess how many shapes there are, then discuss with the group how best to count them, perhaps by matching with cubes then arranging them in groups of, say, tens and ones, fives or twos. Suitable questions are:

❑ Can you estimate the number of shapes on this card?
❑ What would your estimate be to the nearest 10?
❑ Why are some answers different?
❑ How can we find out which answer is closest?
❑ What would be the best way to count the cubes?

##  Make seven

### Objectives

Levels 2, 3:
addition and subtraction
facts to 10 (level 2) or 20
(level 3).

### Organisation

Work with a group of
three or four children.

### Words to stress

More, fewer, difference,
add, plus, take away,
subtract, minus, sum,
total, altogether, equals.

### Preparation

Make four sets of cards numbered from 0 to 5. At level 3,
use a pack of playing cards without the picture cards.

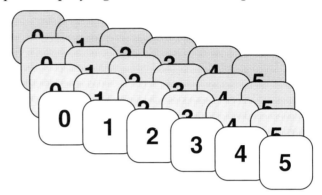

### Procedure

Shuffle the cards. Divide them into two packs and place
these face down on the table. Children take turns to take
a card from each pack, add the two numbers, and decide
what needs to be done to make a final score of 7. For
example, if 2 and 4 are chosen, then 1 must be added. If 4
and 5 are chose, then 2 must be subtracted. During play,
use questions like these, varying the vocabulary.

❐ What is the sum of your two numbers? What do they
total? Is that more or fewer than 7?
❐ What is the difference between 7 and your total?
❐ How will you get to 7? Will you add or subtract?
How many will you add on or take away?
❐ Can you explain how you got that?

After a while, change the target number to, say, 5 or 9.
For another variation, divide the cards into three packs.
For work at level 3, make the target a number like 15.

##  Buttons

### Objectives

Levels 2, 3:
addition and subtraction
facts to 10 (level 2) or 20
(level 3);
counting in twos or fives.

### Preparation

You need three dice and a collection of about 100 buttons.

### Procedure

Children take turns to roll one of the dice. They pick up
that number of buttons.

Ask each child a different question, such as:

**Organisation**
Work with a group of three or four children.

**Words to stress**
More, fewer, difference, add, subtract, minus, sum, total, altogether.

❐ How many more buttons would make a total of 10?
❐ How many fewer than 10 is your number?
❐ What do you need to subtract from 10 to find out?
❐ How many buttons have you collected altogether? Can you estimate the number in your pile?
❐ Can you count them all in twos? In fives?

After a while, change the target to 9 or 11. At level 3, two or even three dice can be rolled and made up to 15 to 20.

## (9) Coins

**Objectives**
Levels 2, 3:
addition of coins to 20p.

**Organisation**
Work with a group of any size, or the whole class.

**Words to stress**
Amount, sum, total, value.

### Preparation
You will need a board or wall-chart on which to keep a record. Some children might find it helpful to have some coins to experiment with, but encourage them to imagine and to calculate mentally as far as possible.

### Procedure
Ask the children:

❐ Which amounts up to 20p can be paid using just one coin? *(1p, 2p, 5p, 10p, 20p)*
❐ Which amounts up to 20p can be paid using just two coins? *(2p, 3p, 4p, 6p, 7p, 10p, 11p, 12p, 15p, 20p)*
❐ Using just three coins? *(3p, 4p, 5p, 6p, 7p, 8p, 9p, 11p, 12p, 13p, 14p, 15p, 16p, 17p, 20p)* Which coins would you use in each case? Is there more than one way for any amount? *(12p = 5p + 5p + 2p or 10p + 1p + 1p)*
❐ Is there a systematic way to keep a record?

Can you make it with just three coins?

| Amount | 1p | 2p | 5p | 10p |
|---|---|---|---|---|
| 1p | | | | |
| 2p | | | | |
| 3p | ✓✓✓ | | | |
| 4p | ✓✓ | ✓ | | |
| 5p | ✓ | ✓✓ | | |
| 6p | | ✓✓✓ | | |
| 7p | ✓✓ | | ✓ | |

❐ Which amounts up to 20p need four or more coins? *(18p and 19p)* Which coins do you need? *(10p, 5p, 2p, 1p and 10p, 5p, 2p, 2p)*
❐ Which coins could you get as change from 10p if you bought something costing 3p? As change from 20p for something costing 14p?

11

# (9) Towers

## Objectives
Levels 2, 3:
add three numbers to total 10 (level 2) or 20 (level 3).

## Organisation
Work with a group of any size.

## Words to stress
More, fewer, add, plus, sum, total, altogether. Arrange, symmetrical.

## Preparation
You need 10 cubes to demonstrate, and a board or large sheet of paper to record the children's results. On another day, use a different number of cubes, say 15.

## Procedure
Tell the children to imagine different ways of arranging 10 cubes into three towers. Show the children one way, then ask:

- ❐ How shall we record the heights of our three towers?
- ❐ Is 3 + 2 + 5 the same as 5 + 3 + 2?
- ❐ Can you imagine three other towers using 10 cubes?
- ❐ How many different ways can you think of? *(8)*
- ❐ How many of the sets of three towers have two the same height? *(4)*
- ❐ Could we record this in a way which is symmetrical? *(4 + 2 + 4, 3 + 4 + 3, 2 + 6 + 2, 1 + 8 + 1)*
- ❐ Can you imagine four towers made from 10 cubes? How many of the sets of four are symmetrical? *(2)*

# (10) Pairs

## Objectives
Levels 2, 3:
addition and subtraction facts to 10 or beyond.

## Organisation
Work with a group of any size.
With a large group answers can be recorded.
With a smaller group answers can be given orally.

## Preparation
Make two cards with a different single-digit number on each side.

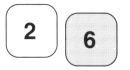 

## Procedure
Put the cards on the table and ask the children to give the total of the two numbers which are face up. Then ask more questions, varying the operation and vocabulary used. Before each question turn over one or both of the cards so that the numbers change. With a larger group the cards can be held up for everyone to see.

Suitable questions to ask are:

*Addition*
- ❏ What is the sum of … and …?
- ❏ What is the total of … and …?
- ❏ How many is … and … altogether?
- ❏ What is … plus …?
- ❏ Add … to …  What does it equal?
- ❏ If you count on … from …, what do you get?
- ❏ What is … more than …?

*Subtraction*
- ❏ What is … minus …?
- ❏ Subtract … from …  What do you get?
- ❏ What is the difference between … and …?
- ❏ How many more than … is …?
- ❏ What should we add to … to make …?
- ❏ What is … fewer than …?
- ❏ When I take … from a number, I get …
  What is the number?

## (11) Straws

### Objectives
Levels 2, 3:
repeated addition to 12 (level 2) or 24 (level 3); division by 2, 3, 4, 5 or 6; partition of 12 or 24.

### Organisation
Work with a small group of, say, three or four children.

### Words to stress
Divide, remainder, add, altogether; triangle, square, pentagon, hexagon, heptagon, octagon.

**Words to stress** (first panel)
One, two, three …
How many?
More, fewer, altogether, total, equals, sum, difference, plus, add, minus, subtract.

### Preparation
You need 12 straws for an introductory demonstration and for checking suggestions, and a board or large sheet of paper for recording.  For level 3, you need 24 straws.

### Procedure
Ask the children to imagine making squares from the 12 straws.  Then ask them:

- ❏ How many squares could you make altogether? *(3)*
- ❏ How many triangles? *(4)*  How many hexagons? *(2)*
- ❏ How many × shapes could you make? *(6)*
- ❏ How many pentagons could you make? *(2)*
  How many sticks would be left over? *(2)*
- ❏ Could you make three different shapes using all 12 straws? *(Cross, square and hexagon; cross, triangle and heptagon; triangle, square and pentagon)*
- ❏ What other combinations of shapes could you make?
- ❏ What if you had 20 straws?

# (12) Bonds

## Objectives
Levels 2, 3:
addition facts to 10 (level 2) or 20 (level 3).

## Organisation
Work with a large group, or the whole class.

## Words to stress
Sum, total, altogether.

## Preparation
Get the children to sit in a large circle. They should be able to see a board or wall-chart for recording purposes.

## Procedure
The first child chooses a number such as 8, and then says it in the form of an addition bond, for example 5 plus 3. Children round the circle then take turns to express 8 as a different addition bond. This continues until no more are suggested. A child who cannot suggest a bond chooses a new number, such as 6, says it as an addition bond, and the game continues. It is helpful to record all suggestions and to get the children to look for patterns. You can ask:

❑ Is 5 + 3 the same as or different from 3 + 5?
❑ Can we record these bonds in a sensible order?
❑ How can we tell if we have said them all?

# (13) Odds and evens

## Objectives
Levels 2, 3:
addition facts to 20; odd and even numbers.

## Organisation
Work with a group of about six children. Children can continue the game independently.

## Words to stress
Sum, total, altogether, odd, even.

## Preparation
Take a pack of playing cards. Remove the picture cards.

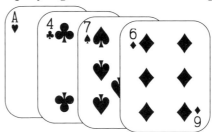

## Procedure
Divide the pack into two stacks placed face down. Turn over cards two at a time, one from each stack, to play *Snap*:

❑ at level 2, for pairs that are both odd (or both even);
❑ at level 3, for pairs that total an odd (or even) number.

Ask questions like:

❑ Is ... odd or even? How can you tell?
❑ Is the sum of two even numbers odd or even?
 What about the sum of two odd numbers?
 And the sum of one odd and one even number?
❑ Are there more even sums? How can you tell?

# (14) Toyshop

## Objectives
Levels 2, 3:
addition and subtraction facts to 10 (level 2) or 20 (level 3);
use of coins.

## Organisation
Work with a group of up to four children.

## Words to stress
Price, cost, amount, sum, total, more, difference.

## Preparation
Collect a set of toys, or pictures of toys pasted on card. Make a set of price tags, varying from about 8p to 20p. You will also need a supply of 1p, 2p, 5p and 10p coins for each child in the group, and a box or 'till' into which the coins can be paid one at a time.

## Procedure
Children take turns to choose a toy and a price tag. The other children in the group then take turns to pay a single coin towards the cost of the toy and to say the total amount paid so far. The child who pays the last coin to make up the exact cost wins the toy. Questions to ask are:

❏ What does this toy cost?
❏ Which coin will you pay?
  What would the total paid then be?
  How much would that leave to pay?
  Would Aziz be able to pay that using just one coin?
  If so, can you use a different coin?
❏ How many coins are needed to pay the difference?
  What is the least number?
❏ Who do you think is likely to win the toy? Why?

The same game can be played with coins of greater value and amounts up to £1.

# (15) Darts

## Objectives
Level 3:
addition and subtraction facts to 20.

## Organisation
Work with a large group, or the whole class.

## Words to stress
More, less, add, subtract, plus, minus, difference.

## Preparation
Draw a simple 1 to 20 'dartboard'.

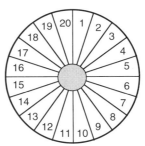

## Procedure
Explain that three darts are thrown and land on three different numbers. The score is, say, 15. Then ask:

❐ How could three darts score 15?
❐ If one of the numbers is 1, what do the other two numbers add up to? (14) What could they be? How shall we record this? Is there a systematic way?
   *(1,2,12;  1,3,11;  1,4,10;  1,5,9;  1,6,8.)*
❐ Are there other possibilities for the three numbers?
   *(2,3,10;  2,4,9;  2,5,8;  2,6,7;  3,4,8;  3,5,7;  4,5,6)*
❐ What if two or more darts land on the same number?
   *(1,1,13;  2,2,11;  3,3,9;  4,4,7;  5,5,5;  6,6,3;  7,7,1)*

# (16) Half a pound

## Objectives
Level 3:
addition of 5p, 10p and 20p coins;
2, 5 and 10 times tables.

## Organisation
Work with a large group, or the whole class. Smaller groups can be formed to work independently, with results compared later.

## Words to stress
More, add, plus, times, multiply, total, equals.

## Preparation
Ask the children to imagine a pile of 5p, 10p and 20p coins.

## Procedure
Explain that the group is to investigate different ways of making 50p. *(There are 12 altogether.)* Ask questions like:

❐ If all the coins are the same, what possibilities are there? *(Ten 5p or five 10p)*
❐ What if all three types of coin are used? *(One 20p, two 10p and two 5p, or one 20p, one 10p and four 5p)*
❐ What if only 20p and 10p coins are used? *(One 20p and three 10p, or two 20p and one 10p)* Only 20p and 5p coins? *(One 20p and six 5p, or two 20p and two 5p)* 10p and 5p coins? *(One 10p and eight 5p, or two 10p and six 5p, or three 10p and four 5p, or four 10p and two 5p)*

#  Biscuits

## Objectives

Level 3:
addition and subtraction
of multiples of 5;
5 and 10 times tables.

## Organisation

Work with a group of any
size.

## Words to stress

More, add, plus, subtract,
minus, difference, times,
multiply, total, equals,
cost, price.

## Preparation

Ask the children to imagine that they have these five
biscuits and a box which will hold just three biscuits.

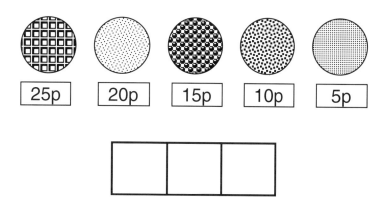

## Procedure

Ask the children questions like:

❏ What is the total cost of all five biscuits? *(75p)*
How did you work that out?
❏ What is the cost of the cheapest box of biscuits? *(30p)*
How did you work that out?
❏ What is the cost of the most expensive box? *(60p)*
How did you work that out?
❏ Which biscuits would be in the box if the cost were
55p? *(25p, 20p, 10p)*
❏ What if the cost were 40p? *(25p, 10p, 5p)*
How did you work that out?
Is there another possibility? *(20p, 15p, 5p)*
❏ If you could use as many of each biscuit as you liked,
what would be the cost of the cheapest box? *(15p)*
Of the most expensive box? *(75p)*
❏ Could you make a box costing 25p? *(10p, 10p, 5p)*
Is there any other possibility? *(5p, 5p, 15p)*
Costing 65p? *(25p, 25p, 15p or 20p, 20p, 25p)*
❏ What would the box cost if each biscuit in it were the
same? *(15p, 30p, 45p, 60p or 75p)*
❏ If the price of the box is 60p, and all three biscuits cost
the same, what does one biscuit cost? *(20p)*
How did you work it out?
❏ If each biscuit in a box is different, how many different
boxes of biscuits could you make? *(10)*
How shall we record it? Is there a systematic way?
What would they cost? *(60p, 55p, 50p, 50p, 45p, 45p,
40p, 40p, 35p, 30p)* How many different prices? *(7)*

# (18) Shopping

## Objectives

Level 3:
addition and subtraction facts to 20; multiplication facts to $5 \times 5$, and the 2, 5 and 10 times tables.

## Organisation

With pictures and prices displayed on a large wall-mounted poster, you can work with the whole class, directing appropriate questions to individuals.
For six to eight children, sit round a table or on the floor, with the items arranged for all to see clearly.

## Words to stress

Price, cost, value, sum, total, more, less, greatest, least, difference.

## Preparation

Label some different small items with a price up to 10p, or stick pictures and prices on card. On another day, use a different selection of objects and prices.

6p   7p   3p   4p   9p

## Procedure

Put questions to individuals, as appropriate.

❑ What would we have to pay for the … and the …?
❑ What is the total cost of the …, the … and the …?
❑ What is the difference in price between the … and the …?
❑ How much more than the … is the …?
❑ What change would we get from 15p if we bought the …?
❑ What change would we get from 20p if we bought the … and the …?
❑ What two things could you buy for exactly …? What other possibilities are there?
❑ Could you buy three things for exactly …? Are there any other possibilities?
❑ What coins could you use to pay exactly …?
   What other possibilities are there?
   What is the least number of coins you need?
   What is the greatest number?
❑ What would five packets of … cost?
❑ What would the … cost if it were ten times as much?
❑ Which costs more, three of the …, or four of the …?

# (19) Three numbers

## Objectives
Level 3:
addition and subtraction facts to 20.

## Organisation
Work with a large group or the whole class.

## Words to stress
More, less, add, subtract, plus, minus, difference.

## Preparation
You need a board or large sheet of paper on which to record children's suggestions.

## Procedure
Choose three numbers, perhaps 3, 5, 7. Use these and the signs + and – to make all the whole numbers from 1 to 10. First find different ways of making 1, then ways of making 2, and so on. Start by using each number only once and then allow numbers and signs to be used as often as you like. As an extension, see how far you can go beyond 10.

# (20) Strips

## Objectives
Levels 3 and 4:
estimation of a length in centimetres;
subtraction facts to 20;
rounding two-digit numbers (level 3);
subtraction of 2 two-digit numbers (level 4).

## Organisation
Work with a large group, or the whole class.

## Words to stress
More, less, longer, shorter, wider, thinner, difference, take away, subtract, minus; estimate, approximate.

## Preparation
You need a board or wall-chart to record suggestions. Cut out ten strips of paper and put them in an open box. For level 3, the lengths of the strips should vary between 10 cm and 20 cm and the width from 1 cm to 10 cm. For level 4, cut lengths up to 100 cm. Mark the back of each strip with the cut length and width in centimetres.

## Procedure
Pull a strip out of the box and hold it up for the children to estimate its length in centimetres. Ask four or five different children for their estimates and write them on the board. Now tell the children the cut length. Ask:

❐ Which estimate was the most (the least) accurate?
❐ By how much did the most and least accurate estimates differ?
❐ Which estimates were within 10 cm?
❐ Which estimates were accurate to the nearest 10 cm?
❐ If my estimate were 7 cm out, what would it have been? What else could it be?
❐ How did you make your estimate?

Repeat with different strips, sometimes asking for an estimate of the width instead of the length. Hold the strips in different positions – vertically, horizontally, sloping. More confident pupils can estimate the total length of two strips or the length of the diagonal.

# (21) Two dice

## Objectives

Levels 3 and 4:
addition and subtraction
of a series of numbers
from 1 to 6;
subtraction of 2 two-digit
numbers.

## Organisation

Work with a group of up
to six children.

## Words to stress

Sum, total, difference,
add, subtract;
faces, opposite, rotate.

## Preparation

You need two dice to demonstrate the investigation or to
check children's responses.

## Procedure

Put questions to the children. Tell them to imagine the
dice and think of the answers rather than referring to the
dice. Encourage systematic recording where it is needed.

❑ What is the total number of spots on one dice? *(21)*
❑ Imagine that I use one dice and throw a ..., what
   number is on the table? *(Opposite faces add to 7)*
   What is the sum of the spots on the five faces showing?
   What if I throw ... instead?
❑ What is the total number of spots on two dice? *(42)*
❑ If I use two dice and throw double 5, how many spots
   are there on the ten faces showing? *(38)*     What if I
   throw ... and ...?
❑ How many different pairs of numbers can be made by
   throwing two dice? *(21, as 3, 4 is the same as 4, 3)*
❑ How many different totals can be made? *(11)*
❑ Which totals occur only once? *(12, 11, 3, 2)*
❑ Which occur most frequently? *(8, 7, 6)* Why?

❑ If I build a tower from two dice, with 4 on the upper
   and 1 on the lower of the two touching faces, how
   many faces would be showing? (9)
   What is the sum of the spots on these faces? *(31)*
   What if ... and ... are the touching faces?
❑ What if I put the dice side by side? How many spots
   would show if 3 and 4 are the touching faces?

#  Letter patterns

## Objectives
Levels 3, 4:
multiples of 2, 3 and 4.

## Organisation
Work with a group of
any size.

## Words to stress
Add, sum, total,
altogether, pattern,
multiple, table,
odd, even.

## Preparation
You need some straws with which to form letters. With a
larger group you could draw on a board instead.

## Procedure
A number of capital letters are made from straight lines.
For example: L, T, V and X are formed from two lines.

One ✕ needs two straws.

Two ✕✕ needs how many straws?

Three ✕✕✕ needs how many straws?

❑ How many straws are needed for five Xs? For eight?
❑ How many Xs if 14 straws are used? 20 straws?
❑ Is there a systematic way to record it? *For example,*

| No. of Xs | 1 | 2 | 3 | 4 | 5 | 6 | 7 |
|-----------|---|---|---|---|----|----|----|
| No. of straws | 2 | 4 | 6 | 8 | 10 | 12 | 14 |

❑ Is there a pattern? Can you continue it?
❑ How many straws are needed to make fifteen Xs? How
did you work it out?
❑ What do the numbers of straws have in common?

Now try letters made from three straight lines. Ask:

❑ What if we tried Y or Z? What is the pattern now?
What do the numbers of straws have in common?
❑ How many straws are needed for ten Ys? 20? 30?

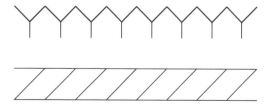

❑ Which other letters give the same number pattern?
*(A, F, I, K)*
❑ What if we tried W or E?

Now try patterns for Ns or Hs, which are different, asking similar questions.

| No. of Ns | 1 | 2 | 3 | 4 | 5 | 6 | 7 |
|---|---|---|---|---|---|---|---|
| No. of straws | 3 | 5 | 7 | 9 | 11 | 13 | 15 |

❐ Why does the N pattern go up in twos?
❐ How many Ns would there be if you used 30 straws, and how many straws would be left? *(14 with one left)*
❐ What if you made Ms? *(9 with two left)*

# ㉓ Bus tickets

## Objectives
Levels 3, 4:
addition of 50p, 20p, 10p, 5p, 2p and 1p coins, to a maximum value of 88p.

## Organisation
Work with a group of any size, or the whole class.

## Words to stress
Amount, sum, total, value, cheap, expensive.

## Preparation
You will need a board or wall-chart on which to keep a record. Children at level 3 might find it helpful to have one of each of the coins to experiment with.

## Procedure
Ask the children to imagine that they have one of each of these coins: 20p, 10p, 5p, 2p, 1p. They need to buy a bus ticket from a machine which does not give change. What are the different tickets that can or cannot be bought?

❐ What is the cheapest ticket you could buy? *(1p)*
  What is the most expensive? *(38p)*
❐ Which tickets could be bought with just one coin?
❐ Which tickets could be bought with just two coins? *(3p, 6p, 7p, 11p, 12p, 15p, 21p, 22p, 25p, 30p)*
❐ What is the smallest amount you could not pay? *(4p)*
❐ Is there a systematic way to keep a record?
  *(One way is to make a table of five columns labelled with each coin, and 38 rows labelled from 1p to 38p. This can be ticked appropriately. All amounts can be made with the exception of 4p, 9p, 14p, 19p, 24p, 29p and 34p.)*
❐ What do you notice about the tickets you can't buy? Can you explain this? *(4p is impossible, hence 9p, etc.)*
❐ What if we added a 50p coin? What is the most expensive ticket you could buy now? *(88p)*
❐ Which tickets can't you buy? *(As above, also 39p, 40p to 49p inclusive, 54p, 59p, 64p, 69p, 74p, 79p and 84p)*

# (24) Perimeters

### Objectives

Level 4:
calculation of the
perimeter of a shape
made from squares;
addition of a series of
single-digit numbers.

### Organisation

Work with a group of
any size, or the whole
class.

### Words to stress

Area, perimeter;
sum, total.

## Preparation

Each child needs some squared paper. With a small group
it helps to have 16 square tiles to demonstrate with.

## Procedure

Show the children a shape made from 16 squares touching
edge to edge. Remind them of the definition of perimeter,
and ask them to calculate it for the shapes you have made.
Aim to add groups of numbers such as 2 + 3 + 2 + 4 and
avoid simply counting individual squares along each side.

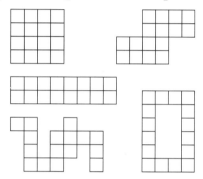

Now ask the children to imagine other shapes that could
be made from 16 tiles, using their squared paper to help.
You can ask questions like these.

❐ Imagine a rectangle made from 16 tiles. How long is it?
How wide is it? What is its perimeter?

❐ Could you make another rectangle with a longer
(shorter) perimeter?

❐ Could you make an L-shape from two rectangles?
How many tiles would you use for the first rectangle?
For the second? What is the length of the perimeter?

❐ Still keeping those numbers of tiles for each of your
rectangles for your L-shape, can you make one of the
rectangles different? What is the perimeter now?

❐ Can you rearrange your two rectangles to make a
T-shape? Does the perimeter alter?

❐ What other L-shapes and T-shapes can you make?
What about shapes from three rectangles like U-shapes
or I-shapes or H-shapes? What is the perimeter each
time?

❐ How many different perimeters have we got?
Which is the longest? Which is the shortest?

❐ What if we allowed shapes with one hole in? With two
holes in? Can you make any with a longer perimeter
than we already have?

# 25 Desert island

## Objectives
Level 4:
mutiplication facts up to
5 × 5 and 5 × 6;
addition and subtraction
of 2 two-digit numbers.

## Organisation
Work with a group of
any size, or the whole
class. The class can be
divided into smaller
groups to work on
certain numbers, with
results collected later.

## Words to stress
Sum, difference, product,
multiple.

## Preparation
You will need a board or wall-chart on which to keep a
record.

## Procedure
Tell the children to imagine themselves marooned on an
island. All they have to measure with are five 5 metre and
five 6 metre bamboo rods. They need to measure all
distances from 1 to 40 metres in order to build themselves
a shelter. The challenge is, can they do it?

Suitable questions to ask are:

❒ If we just used one rod, which distances could we
measure? *(5 m and 6 m)*
❒ If we used two rods? *(10 m, 11 m, 12 m and also 1 m)*

*In discussing two rods, you will need to establish that there are
two ways of measuring. The simplest way is to place rods end
to end and find the total distance. A second way is to place one
set of rods laid end to end next to another set placed end to end,
and to find the difference between the two sets.*

Continue by asking:

❒ How shall we keep a record?
❒ Is there a systematic way to investigate?
❒ If you can measure 11 metres, what other distances
can you measure? *(16 m, 21 m, 26 m, 31 m by using more
5 m rods, 17 m, 23 m, 29 m, 35 m by using more 6 m rods, or
22 m and 33 m by adding more pairs of 5 m and 6 m rods ...)*
❒ Is there any distance you can't measure? *(36 m)*
❒ How far can you go beyond 40 metres?
❒ What if you had 5 metre and 7 metre rods instead?

# (26) Links

## Objectives

Level 4:
addition of a series of single digits.

## Organisation

Work with a group of any size, or the whole class. Children could follow this activity by creating their own grids and exploring them.

## Words to stress

Sum, total.

## Preparation

Draw a 4 × 4 grid on a board or wall-chart or worksheet, and fill it randomly with single digit numbers.

| 8—5 | 6 | 9 |
|---|---|---|---|
| 4 | 3—8 | 1 |
| 5 | 7 | 2 | 5 |
| 6 | 5 | 9 | 6 |

## Procedure

Explain that the children are to link any four numbers and add them up. The links can go straight up or down or across, but not diagonally. One example is 24, because 8 + 5 + 3 + 8 = 24. Then ask:

❐ What other totals can you make?

After a while, ask:

❐ What is the greatest possible total? *(8 + 5 + 6 + 9 = 28)*
❐ What is the smallest possible total? *(1 + 5 + 2 + 7 = 15)*
❐ What if only diagonal links are allowed?
    *(Greatest: 9 + 8 + 7 + 9 = 33   Smallest: 1 + 2 + 3 + 5 = 11)*

---

# (27) Six by six

## Objectives

Level 4:
multiplication facts to 10 × 10.

## Organisation

Work with a group of about six children around a table. Each member of the group needs to see the array of cards clearly.

## Preparation

You need a pack of playing cards with the picture cards and aces removed. Deal them face up in an 6 × 6 array.

**Words to stress**

Mutiply, product.

## Procedure

Secretly choose two cards that are next to each other in either a row or a column. Tell the children the product of the two numbers. The first to point to any two touching cards that give the same product wins them and takes them from the array. Continue until all possible pairs of cards have been won. (Regroup the cards if too many gaps appear.) During play, ask questions like:

❐ Which pair of cards has a product of 36?
❐ Which two numbers when multiplied make 16?

Children can continue to play by themselves. The dealer chooses the first product. The winner of the pair of cards chooses the next product.

## (28) Four in a row

**Objectives**

Level 4:
addition and subtraction of 2 two-digit numbers.

**Organisation**

Work with a group of any size, or the whole class.

**Words to stress**

Sum, total, difference.

### Preparation

Draw this grid on a board or wall-chart. You need two coloured pens or coloured chalk to mark the numbers.

| 13 | 93 | 53 | 32 | 66 |
|----|----|----|----|----|
| 70 | 23 | 85 | 19 | 37 |
| 99 | 81 | 15 | 75 | 17 |
| 18 | 62 | 46 | 31 | 84 |
| 47 | 14 | 79 | 98 | 28 |

Underneath it, write this list of numbers.

19    28    34    47    51    65

### Procedure

Form two teams. The teams take turns to try to make one of the numbers on the grid by finding the sum or the difference of any pair of the listed numbers. The number is then coloured. The winner is the first team to make four numbers in a straight line. During play ask:

❐ Which number can you make? How did you work that out? Did you add or subtract?
❐ Is that the best position to go for?
❐ Can you make any numbers that are not on the grid? (4, 6, 9, 112, 116)

# Part 3: Puzzles and games

These number activities are intended for children to work on independently without aids like counters, pencil and paper or a calculator. Most will take from 15 to 20 minutes to complete, assuming that games are played several times. The puzzles are for individual children to work on at school or at home, and several of them can be used more than once. The games are for two or more children to play together.

The games and puzzles provide situations for children to think logically. They offer good opportunities for planning, predicting, learning from mistakes or unproductive moves, spotting a successful strategy and pursuing it, and so on. Where it is appropriate you could ask children to:

- consider the possible opening moves and which is the best;
- consider the positions possible after one, two or three moves;
- devise ways of recording patterns of moves;
- find the least number of moves needed;
- predict and then test who will win the game;
- consider whether a draw is a possibility;
- show that something is impossible;
- talk or write about winning and losing strategies;
- alter the rules in some way in order to see what happens;
- extend the puzzle or game and try to generalise it.

Besides offering ample opportunities for children to use and apply mathematics, the puzzles and games also:

- provide varied contexts for children to practise quick recall of number facts and mental arithmetic skills;
- allow you to assess their progress by observing what they do and listening to what they say.

Some of the evidence you might look for as children undertake these activities is:

- growing confidence as indicated by the questions children ask: for example, 'Shall I try ... ?' compared with 'What shall I do now?';
- the speed and accuracy of their recall;
- their ability to talk clearly about what they have been doing, to you or to their class-mates, or to write about or record their work in some way;
- their ability to persevere in finding solutions;
- their willingness to work cooperatively with others.

The level of difficulty and the skills required in each of the puzzles and games, with solutions to the puzzles, are given in the notes on pages 60 to 62.

Name:

Choose three of these numbers to fill each set of boxes.

# 1 2 3 4 5 6 7 8 9

Use three different numbers each time.

□ + □ = □         □ + □ = □

□ + □ = □         □ + □ = □

□ + □ = □         □ + □ = □

□ + □ = □         □ + □ = □

□ + □ = □         □ + □ = □

□ + □ = □         □ + □ = □

□ + □ = □         □ + □ = □

□ + □ = □         □ + □ = □

Name:

Put 1, 2 or 3 in each circle.
Make each side add to 5.

Do it in different ways.

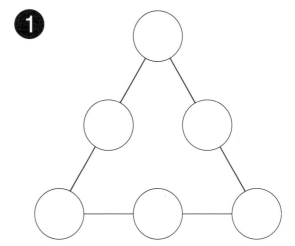

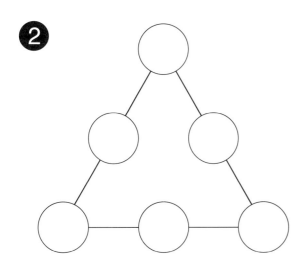

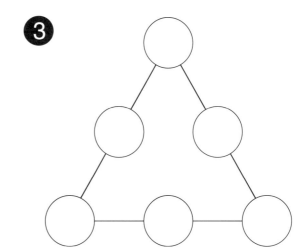

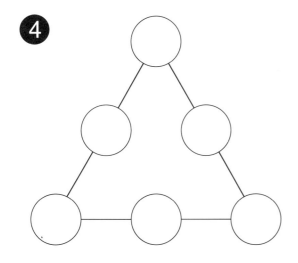

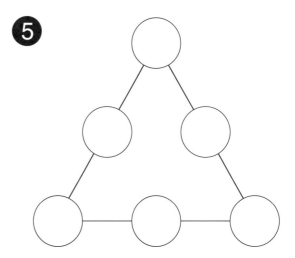

# (3) Presents

You have lots of 1p, 2p and 5p coins to buy ten presents.
Each present costs 10p. Draw 10p in different ways.

From *Mental Maths* Anita Straker © Cambridge University Press 1994

## (4) Target

Name:

Use only these numbers and signs.

| 1 | 4 | 5 | + | − |

Make these numbers. You can use the same number twice.

1 = ☐ ☐ ☐

2 = ☐ ☐ ☐

3 = ☐ ☐ ☐

4 = ☐ ☐ ☐

5 = ☐ ☐ ☐

6 = ☐ ☐ ☐

8 = ☐ ☐ ☐

9 = ☐ ☐ ☐

10 = ☐ ☐ ☐

From *Mental Maths* Anita Straker © Cambridge University Press 1994

**Signs**

Name:

Choose a sign to put in each box.

| = | − | + |

Make each sum correct.

| 3 | | 2 | | 1 | | 6 |

| 8 | | 1 | | 3 | | 4 |

| 5 | | 2 | | 3 | | 4 |

| 7 | | 2 | | 1 | | 6 |

| 5 | | 3 | | 2 | | 4 |

| 2 | | 5 | | 1 | | 8 |

| 6 | | 4 | | 9 | | 1 |

| 8 | | 6 | | 7 | | 9 |

| 5 | | 3 | | 2 | | 0 |

   From *Mental Maths* Anita Straker © Cambridge University Press 1994

Imagine throwing three dice.

**1** What three numbers would give you a total of 7? Investigate different ways of doing it.

☐ + ☐ + ☐          ☐ + ☐ + ☐

☐ + ☐ + ☐          ☐ + ☐ + ☐

**2** What three numbers would give you a total of 9?

☐ + ☐ + ☐          ☐ + ☐ + ☐

☐ + ☐ + ☐          ☐ + ☐ + ☐

☐ + ☐ + ☐          ☐ + ☐ + ☐

Name:

**1** Try any two numbers.

4

9     6

8

The biggest sum is: ☐

The smallest sum is: ☐

The biggest difference is: ☐

The smallest difference is: ☐

**2** Put your own numbers in the boxes.  Try any two of them.

☐

☐     ☐

☐

The biggest sum is: ☐

The smallest sum is: ☐

The biggest difference is: ☐

The smallest difference is: ☐

  From *Mental Maths* Anita Straker © Cambridge University Press 1994

Name:

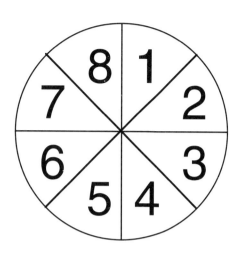

You have three darts.
Each dart must go on the board.
More than one dart can go on a number.

Write a total to aim for such as 12, 13 or 14.

Investigate different ways of scoring your total.

☐ + ☐ + ☐          ☐ + ☐ + ☐

☐ + ☐ + ☐          ☐ + ☐ + ☐

☐ + ☐ + ☐          ☐ + ☐ + ☐

☐ + ☐ + ☐          ☐ + ☐ + ☐

☐ + ☐ + ☐          ☐ + ☐ + ☐

Name:

**1** Make each line add up to 13.

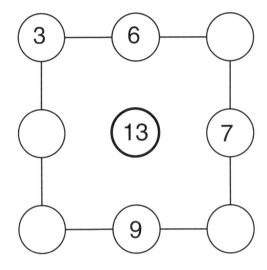

**2** Make each line add up to 17.

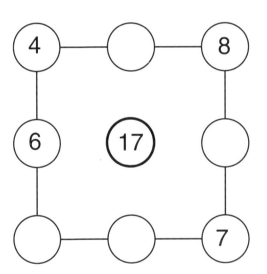

**3** Make each line add up to 20.

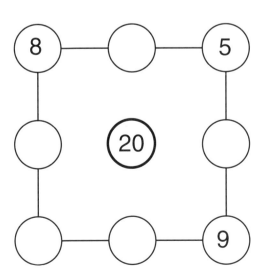

From *Mental Maths* Anita Straker © Cambridge University Press 1994

**1** Use each of the numbers 1 to 8.
Put one number in each box.
Make each side add up to 13.

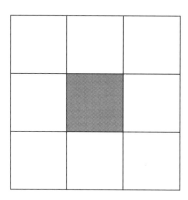

Now do it a different way.

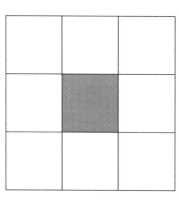

**2** Make each side add up to 14.

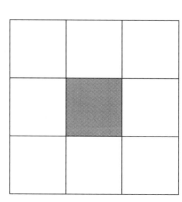

Now do it a different way.

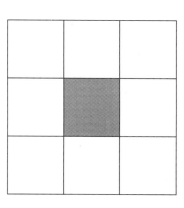

 | 1 | 2 | 3 | 4 | 5 | 6 | 7 | 8 |

From *Mental Maths* Anita Straker © Cambridge University Press 1994

## (11) Make 20

Name:

Put a different small number in each of the two empty boxes.
Put 2 and 3, or 3 and 4, or 2 and 5, or 3 and 5.

| | | + | − | × |
|---|---|---|---|---|

Use the numbers and signs as many times as you like,
but use as few as possible.
Try to make each of the numbers from 1 to 20.

| 1 | | | 11 | |
|---|---|---|---|---|
| 2 | | | 12 | |
| 3 | | | 13 | |
| 4 | | | 14 | |
| 5 | | | 15 | |
| 6 | | | 16 | |
| 7 | | | 17 | |
| 8 | | | 18 | |
| 9 | | | 19 | |
| 10 | | | 20 | |

Were any numbers impossible?

From *Mental Maths* Anita Straker © Cambridge University Press 1994

# (12) Sums

Name:

**1** Use only these numbers.

 (11)  (8)  (19)  (17)

Put a number in each box to make each sum correct.

| ☐ + ☐ = 25 | ☐ – ☐ = 6 |
| ☐ + ☐ = 27 | ☐ – ☐ = 11 |
| ☐ + ☐ = 19 | ☐ – ☐ = 8 |
| ☐ + ☐ = 30 | ☐ – ☐ = 2 |
| ☐ + ☐ = 28 | ☐ – ☐ = 9 |

**2** Write a number less than 20 in each circle.

Use your four numbers to make up some sums.
Use a different pair of numbers each time.

| ☐ + ☐ = ☐ | ☐ – ☐ = ☐ |
| ☐ + ☐ = ☐ | ☐ – ☐ = ☐ |
| ☐ + ☐ = ☐ | ☐ – ☐ = ☐ |

**Pegs**

Name:

The pegs on each line make a pattern.
Fill in the missing numbers.

**1**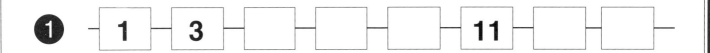

| 1 | 3 | | | | 11 | | |

**2**

| | 4 | | | 10 | | | |

**3**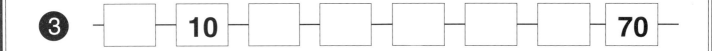

| | 10 | | | | | | 70 |

**4**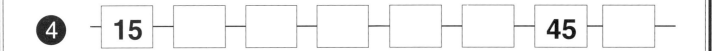

| 15 | | | | | 45 | |

**5**

| | 6 | | | 15 | | | |

**6**

| 90 | | | | | | 20 |

**7**

| | | 50 | | 40 | | | |

**8**

| 2 | | | 11 | | | | |

**9**

| | 21 | | | | 11 | |

From *Mental Maths* Anita Straker © Cambridge University Press 1994

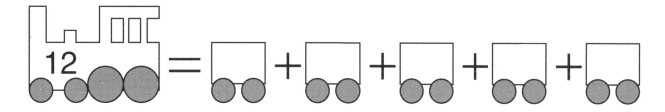

# (14) Trains

Name:

**1** Put 2 or 3 on each truck to make 12.

12 = ☐ + ☐ + ☐ + ☐ + ☐

**2** Put 2 or 5 on each truck to make 13.

13 = ☐ + ☐ + ☐ + ☐ + ☐

**3** Put 3 or 4 on each truck to make 17.

17 = ☐ + ☐ + ☐ + ☐ + ☐

**4** Put 4 or 5 on each truck to make 22.

22 = ☐ + ☐ + ☐ + ☐ + ☐

From *Mental Maths* Anita Straker © Cambridge University Press 1994

Name:

The numbers in the circles have been added in pairs.

The sum of each pair is in the box between the circles.

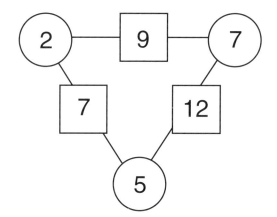

Complete these.

**1**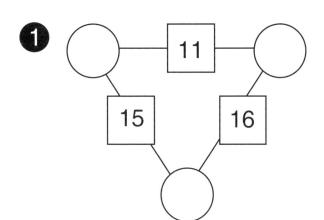

**2**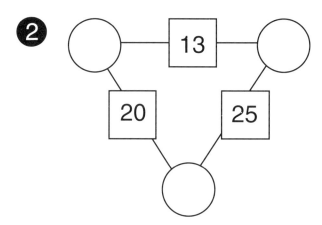

**3**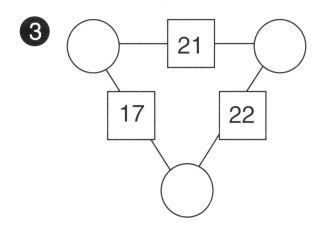

**4**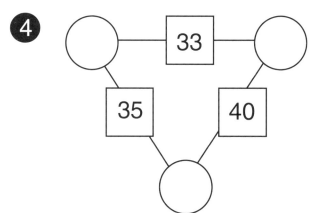

From *Mental Maths* Anita Straker © Cambridge University Press 1994

## 16  Boxes

Name:

**1**  Use only these numbers.

| 17 | 28 | 29 | 37 | 43 |
|----|----|----|----|----|

Put a number in each box to make each sum correct.

☐ − ☐ = 6 　　　 ☐ + ☐ = 45

☐ − ☐ = 8 　　　 ☐ + ☐ = 65

☐ + ☐ = 80 　　　 ☐ − ☐ = 11

☐ − ☐ = 20 　　　 ☐ − ☐ = 26

☐ − ☐ = 9 　　　 ☐ + ☐ = 71

☐ + ☐ = 54 　　　 ☐ − ☐ = 15

**2**  Use the same numbers.  Write four more sums.
The answers should be different from those above.

☐ + ☐ = ☐ 　　　 ☐ − ☐ = ☐

☐ + ☐ = ☐ 　　　 ☐ − ☐ = ☐

Name:

| 33 | 21 | 48 | 37 |
|----|----|----|----|
| 50 | 44 | 31 | 19 |
| 23 | 17 | 35 | 46 |

Pick three different numbers from the grid and add them up.
Investigate different ways of making 100.

☐ + ☐ + ☐          ☐ + ☐ + ☐

☐ + ☐ + ☐          ☐ + ☐ + ☐

☐ + ☐ + ☐          ☐ + ☐ + ☐

☐ + ☐ + ☐          ☐ + ☐ + ☐

☐ + ☐ + ☐          ☐ + ☐ + ☐

☐ + ☐ + ☐          ☐ + ☐ + ☐

From *Mental Maths* Anita Straker © Cambridge University Press 1994

Name:

Write the products of pairs of consecutive numbers.

$1 \times 2$ = ☐

$2 \times 3$ = ☐

$3 \times 4$ = ☐

$4 \times 5$ = ☐

$5 \times 6$ = ☐

$6 \times 7$ = ☐

$7 \times 8$ = ☐

$8 \times 9$ = ☐

$9 \times 10$ = ☐

Describe the pattern made by the products.

Use the pattern to complete these.

$10 \times 11$ = ☐

$11 \times 12$ = ☐

$12 \times 13$ = ☐

$13 \times 14$ = ☐

From *Mental Maths* Anita Straker © Cambridge University Press 1994

Name:

Look for patterns.  Fill in the missing numbers.

$$32 \quad \times \quad 25$$

$$= \quad 16 \quad \times \quad 50$$

$$= \quad \boxed{\phantom{00}} \quad \times \quad 100$$

$$= \quad 4 \quad \times \quad \boxed{\phantom{00}}$$

$$= \quad \boxed{\phantom{00}} \quad \times \quad \boxed{\phantom{00}}$$

$$= \quad \boxed{\phantom{00}} \quad \times \quad \boxed{\phantom{00}}$$

Use the pattern.  What is $32 \times 25$?

Describe how you used the pattern to find your answer.

From *Mental Maths* Anita Straker © Cambridge University Press 1994

The number 18 is twice the sum of its two digits.

$$18 = 2 \times (1 + 8)$$

The number 27 is three times the sum of its two digits.

$$27 = 3 \times (2 + 7)$$

Which two-digit numbers are:

four times the sum of their digits;

five times the sum of their digits;

six times the sum of their digits;

seven times the sum of their digits;

eight times the sum of their digits;

nine times the sum of their digits?

What do all these numbers have in common?

Name:

Choose your stamps:

three of ☐ p and two of ☐ p.

What parcels could you send without buying more stamps?

| Stamps | Total value |
|---|---|
|  |  |
|  |  |
|  |  |
|  |  |
|  |  |
|  |  |
|  |  |
|  |  |
|  |  |
|  |  |
|  |  |

From *Mental Maths* Anita Straker © Cambridge University Press 1994

Name:

Write a number in this box. ☐

Make up 'sums'. Each answer should equal your number.

**1** Use at least one + sign in each of these.

☐ ☐

☐ ☐

**2** Use at least one − sign in each of these.

☐ ☐

☐ ☐

**3** Use at least one × sign in each of these.

☐ ☐

☐ ☐

**4** Use at least one ÷ sign in each of these.

☐ ☐

☐ ☐

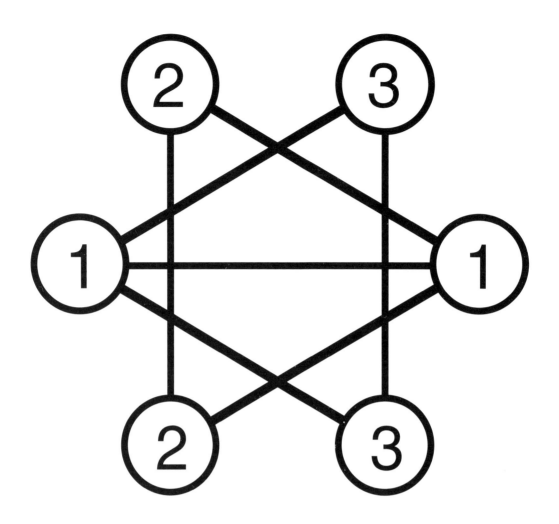

## Rules

You need a counter.

One player puts the counter on a number and says it.

Now take turns.
Slide the counter along a line to another number.
Add on that number and say the new total.

The winner is the one to make the total exactly 17.

If you go over 17 you lose the game.

From *Mental Maths* Anita Straker © Cambridge University Press 1994

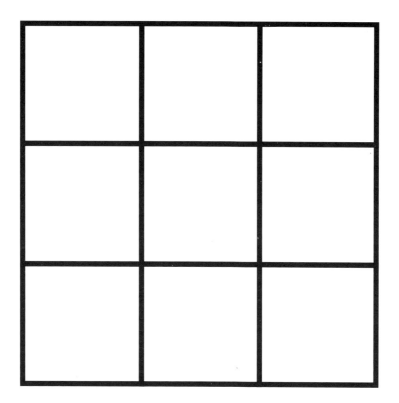

## Rules

You need five 2p and five 5p coins,
and pencil and paper to keep the score.

Take turns to go first.

In turn, choose a coin and put it on the grid.
If you make a line of three coins totalling 9p you score a point.

The winner is the one with most points when each square
has a coin in it.

For a change, try to make lines of 12p.

From *Mental Maths* Anita Straker © Cambridge University Press 1994

## 3 Fill it up

A game for two players

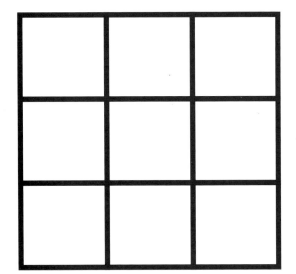 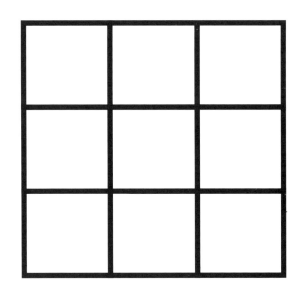

**Rules**

You need a pencil and two dice.

Use one grid each.

Take turns to throw both dice.
Add or subtract the two numbers.
Write the sum or difference in any space on your grid.
Carry on until each grid is full of numbers.

Now take turns to throw the dice again.
If you can, cross out the sum or difference of the numbers.

The winner is the first to cross out all their numbers.

From *Mental Maths* Anita Straker © Cambridge University Press 1994

| | | |
|---|---|---|
| 1 | 5 | 3 |
| 7 | 0 | 8 |
| 4 | 6 | 2 |

| | | |
|---|---|---|
| 1 | 5 | 3 |
| 7 | 0 | 8 |
| 4 | 6 | 2 |

**Rules**

You need two dice and about 20 counters.

Use one grid each.

Take turns to roll the two dice.

Make a number on your grid with the two numbers.
You can add, subtract, multiply or divide them.

Cover the number you made with a counter.

The winner is the first to cover up all their numbers.

From *Mental Maths* Anita Straker © Cambridge University Press 1994

**Make 15**

A game for two players

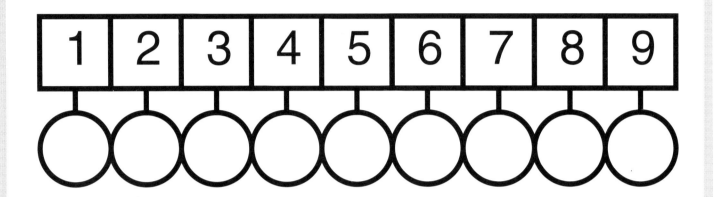

**Rules**

Each player needs five small counters of their own colour. Take turns to go first.

In turn, put a counter in a circle.

Only one counter can be put in each circle.

The winner is the first player to get **three** of their own counters next to numbers that add up to 15.

You might need to place **four or more** of your counters before three of them total 15.

From *Mental Maths* Anita Straker © Cambridge University Press 1994

## 6 ) Take three

A game for two or four players

| 12 | 16 | 20 | 13 | 18 | 22 |
|----|----|----|----|----|----|
| 17 | 11 | 14 | 19 | 23 | 15 |
| 19 | 15 | 9  | 20 | 18 | 21 |
| 22 | 13 | 16 | 24 | 14 | 17 |
| 17 | 10 | 18 | 15 | 11 | 19 |
| 20 | 14 | 12 | 21 | 13 | 16 |

**Rules**

Each team needs some counters of their own colour.
Take turns to choose any **three** of these numbers.

**3   6   4   7   9   2   8   5**

Add them up to make a number on the board.
Cover the number with one of your counters.

The winner is the first team to get four of their counters in a straight line in any direction.

| 2 | 3 | 4 | 5 | 6 |
|---|---|---|---|---|
| 7 | 8 | 9 | 10 | 11 |
| 12 | 13 | 14 | 15 | 16 |
| 17 | 18 | 19 | 20 | 21 |

**Rules**

You need three dice.
Each player needs some counters of their own colour.

Take turns to roll the three dice.
Make a number on the board with the three numbers
and cover it with one of your counters.

You can add, subtract, multiply or divide the numbers,
or use them as tens and units.
For example, with 2, 3 and 5 you could make:
$10 = 2 + 3 + 5$, or $13 = 2 \times 5 + 3$, or $18 = 23 - 5$.

The winner is the one with most counters on the board
when all the squares are full.

From *Mental Maths* Anita Straker © Cambridge University Press 1994

**Make 24**

A game for two players

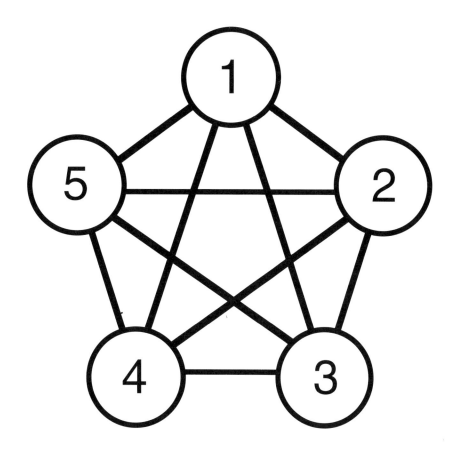

**Rules**

You need a counter.
Take turns to go first.

One player puts the counter on a number and says it.

Now take turns.
Slide the counter along a line to another number.
Add on that number and say the new total.

The winner is the player to make the total exactly 24.

For a change, choose a different total to aim for.

**Luk tsut K'i** A game for two players

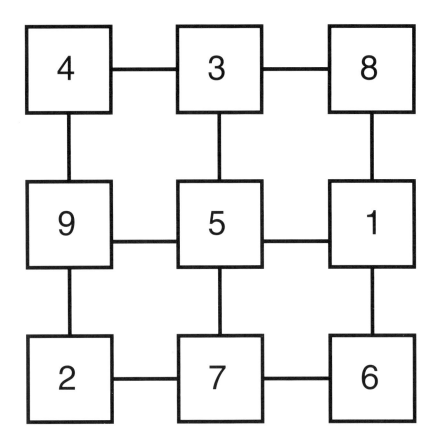

**Rules**

This game is based on one played in China.
Each player needs three counters of their own colour.

Take turns to put one of your counters on a number.
When all six counters are placed, take turns to slide one of
your counters along a line to the next uncovered number.

The game ends when one player has three counters in a
horizontal or vertical straight line.
This player scores 25 points.
The other player scores the sum of the numbers on which
their counters are placed.

The winner is the one with most points after four games.

**Make 30**  A game for two players

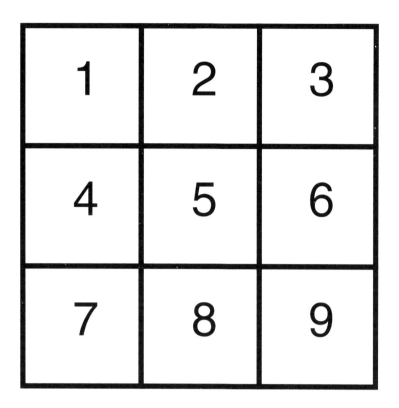

## Rules

You need nine counters between you.

One player puts a counter on any number and says it.

Take turns to put another counter on an uncovered number. Either add or subtract that number and say the new total.

Only one counter can be put on each number.

The winner is the player to reach exactly 30 with any counter. If neither player reaches 30, the winner is the one nearest to 30 with their last counter.

From *Mental Maths* Anita Straker © Cambridge University Press 1994

# Notes on the puzzles and games

1    Trios             Addition facts to 9.

                              1+2=3    1+3=4    1+4=5    1+5=6    1+6=7    1+7=8    1+8=9    2+3=5

                              2+4=6    2+5=7    2+6=8    2+7=9    3+4=7    3+5=8    3+6=9    4+5=9

2    Five-a-side        Addition of 1, 2 and 3 in different ways to total 5.

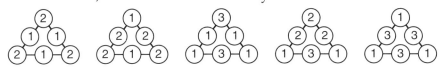

3    Presents          Addition of 1p, 2p and 5p to total 10p.

                              10×1p       8×1p+2p     6×1p+2×2p     4×1p+3×2p     2×1p+4×2p

                              5×2p         2×5p         5p+2×2p+1p    5p+2p+3×1p    5p+5×1p

4    Target             Addition or subtraction of 1, 4 and 5 to total up to 10.

                              1=5–4    2=1+1    3=4–1    4=5–1    5=1+4    6=1+5    8=4+4    9=4+5    10=5+5

5    Signs              Sum or difference of single digits to total up to 10.

                              For example,     3+2+1=6       8–1–3=4          5+2=3+4         7=2–1+6

                              5–3+2=4            2+5+1=8       6+4–9=1          8–6+7=9         5–3–2=0

                              Other solutions are possible.

6    Make 9           Addition of three digits from 1 to 6 to total 7 or 9.

                              1, 1, 5;     1, 2, 4;     1, 3, 3;     2, 2, 3.

                              1, 2, 6;     1, 3, 5;     1, 4, 4;     2, 2, 5;     2, 3, 4;     3, 3, 3.

7    Pairs             Addition and subtraction facts to 20.

                              Biggest sum: 17       Smallest: 10      Biggest difference: 5    Smallest: 1

8    Darts             Addition of three digits from 1 to 8 to total 12, 13 or 14.

                              For 12, there are 10 combinations:        2, 2, 8;     3, 3, 6;     4, 4, 4;

                              5, 5, 2;     1, 3, 8;     1, 4, 7;     1, 5, 6;     2, 3, 7;     2, 4, 6;     3, 4, 5.

                              For 13, there are 10 combinations. For 14, there are 10 combinations.

9    Lines             Addition of three single digits to total 13, 17 or 20.

**10 Sides** — Addition of three single digits to total 13 or 14.

| 6 | 3 | 4 |
|---|---|---|
| 2 |   | 8 |
| 5 | 7 | 1 |

| 2 | 3 | 8 |
|---|---|---|
| 6 |   | 4 |
| 5 | 7 | 1 |

| 7 | 6 | 1 |
|---|---|---|
| 3 |   | 5 |
| 4 | 2 | 8 |

| 3 | 6 | 5 |
|---|---|---|
| 7 |   | 1 |
| 4 | 2 | 8 |

**11 Make 20** — Number bonds to 20. Multiplication facts to 5 × 5.

With 2 and 3, 3 and 4, 2 and 5, or 3 and 5 all numbers from 1 to 20 can be made without using the × sign, often in several different ways. The × sign can be used to replace expressions like 3+3+3 with 3×3.

**12 Sums** — Sums and differences of pairs of numbers up to 30.

8+17=25    8+19=27    8+11=19    11+19=30    11+17=28
17−11=6    19−8=11    19−11=8    19−17=2    17−8=9

**13 Pegs** — Repeated addition or subtraction of 2, 3, 5 or 10.

1, 3, 5, 7, 9, 11 ...          2, 4, 6, 8, 10, 12 ...          0, 10, 20, 30, 40, 50 ...
15, 20, 25, 30, 35 ...        3, 6, 9, 12, 15, 18 ...        90, 80, 70, 60, 50, 40 ...
60, 55, 50, 45, 40 ...        2, 5, 8, 11, 14, 17 ...        23, 21, 19, 17, 15, 13 ...

**14 Trains** — Multiplication facts to 5 × 5. Addition facts to 20.

12=2+2+2+3+3;    13=5+2+2+2+2;    17=3+3+3+4+4;    22=5+5+4+4+4.

## Level 4

**15 Triangles** — Addition and subtraction of one- and two-digit numbers.

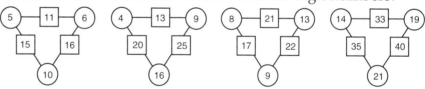

**16 Boxes** — Addition and subtraction of 2 two-digit numbers.

43 − 37 = 6        17 + 28 = 45
37 − 29 = 8        37 + 28 = 65        For others, choose from:
37 + 43 = 80       28 − 17 = 11        17 + 29 = 46        17 + 43 = 60
37 − 17 = 20       43 − 17 = 26        29 + 37 = 66        29 + 43 = 72
37 − 28 = 9        28 + 43 = 71        28 + 29 = 57        43 − 29 = 14
37 + 17 = 54       43 − 28 = 15        29 − 28 = 1         29 − 17 = 12

**17 Make 100** — Addition of two-digit numbers; subtraction from 100.

17, 33, 50;   17, 35, 48;   17, 37, 46;   19, 35, 46;   19, 33, 48;   19, 31, 50;
19, 37, 44;   21, 31, 48;   21, 33, 46;   21, 35, 44;   23, 31, 46;   23, 33, 44.

**18 Patterns 1** — Multiplication facts to 10 × 10.

The pattern of differences is 4, 6, 8, 10, 12, 14, 16, 18, all multiples of 2. The next differences will be 20, 22, 24, 26. Adding on these from 90 gives:   10 × 11 = 110    11 × 12 = 132    12 × 13 = 156    13 × 14 = 182.

| 19 | Patterns 2 | Doubling from 25 and halving from 32. |
|---|---|---|
| | | The pattern is found by halving the left-hand column and doubling the right-hand column, giving $32 \times 25 = 800$. |

| 20 | Digit sums | Multiplication facts to $10 \times 12$. |
|---|---|---|
| | | 12, 24, 36 and 48 are four times the sum of their digits. |
| | | 45 is five times and 54 is six times the sum of its digits. |
| | | 21, 42, 63 and 84 are seven times the sum of their digits. |
| | | 72 is eight times and 81 is nine times the sum of its digits. |
| | | All are multiples of three. |

### Levels 2, 3 or 4

| 21 | Parcels | Multiplication by 2 or 3.  Addition of numbers. |
|---|---|---|
| | | Stamps to choose, for example, could be 2p and 5p (level 2), 15p and 20p (level 3), 14p and 17p (level 4), but any others will do. There are 11 possible combinations if the stamps are a and b: 3a, 2a, a, 2b, b, 3a+2b, 3a+b, 2a+2b, 2a+b, a+2b, a+b. |

| 22 | Inventions | Use of the four rules. |
|---|---|---|

# The games

### Level 2

| 1 | Make 17 | Addition of 1, 2 and 3 to total 17. |
|---|---|---|
| 2 | Nine pence | Addition of three 2p and 5p coins to total 9p or 12p. |
| 3 | Fill it up | Addition of pairs from 1 to 6 to total up to 12. |
| 4 | Cover up | Use of +, −, ×, ÷ and pairs from 1 to 6 to make up to 8. |

### Level 3

| 5 | Make 15 | Addition of  three single digits to total 15. |
|---|---|---|
| 6 | Take three | Addition of three single digits to total from 9 to 24. |
| 7 | Three dice | Use of +, −, ×, ÷ and digits from 1 to 6 to make from 2 to 21. |

### Level 4

| 8 | Make 24 | Addition of a series of digits from 1 to 5 to total 30. |
|---|---|---|
| 9 | Luk tsut K'i | Addition of three two-digit numbers from 1 to 20. |
| 10 | Make 30 | Addition or subtraction of a series of single digits to total 30. |

# Answers: *Mental maths 1*

*Mental Maths 1* involves addition and subtraction facts to 10, and then to 20. This extends to sums like 20 + 40, 24 + 10 or 20 + 3 and differences such as 50 – 30, 38 – 10 or 30 – 2. Multiplication and division in the range 0-20, and by 10 up to 10 × 10, are included. The tasks cover ordinal numbers, place value of tens and units, rounding to the nearest 10, odd and even numbers, simple halves and quarters, telling the time (o'clock and half-past), days of the week and months of the year, use of coins to 20p, estimates with common metric measures (cm, m, kg, l) and recognition of 2D shapes.

## Task 1a
1  8
2  5
3  8
4  5
5  8
6  8
7  6
8  3
9  14
10  3

## Task 1b
1  6 sweets
2  4 is even
3  White triangle
4  7 days
5  7 skittles
6  10
7  9p
8  7p
9  2 cakes
10  3 hours

## Task 1c
1  S
2  Q
3  U
4  A
5  R
6  E

## Task 1d
1  10
2  4
3  12
4  6
5  2
6  3 dots
7  8
8  5
9  7
10  3

## Task 2a
1  4 o'clock
2  April
3  6 years old
4  Black
5  2p
6  13 is odd
7  The square
8  5 marbles
9  4 toffees
10  3

## Task 2b
1  4
2  5
3  2
4  9
5  8
6  6 cm is less
7  19
8  1
9  10
10  5p and 2p

## Task 2c
1  3
2  10
3  10
4  2
5  16 is even
6  20
7  6
8  9
9  2
10  3

## Task 2d
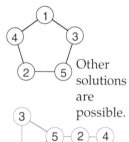

Other solutions are possible.

## Task 3a
1  11
2  4 corners
3  5p and 5p
4  2 hours
5  Black
6  10 toes
7  4p more
8  Thursday
9  3 and 5
10  3 apples

## Task 3b
1  Kelly
2  Ian
3  Ann
4  Carol
5  Lisa
6  3 years
7  Ian
8  Ram
9  3 years
10  4 years old

## Task 3c
1  11 is odd
2  Saturday
3  12
4  Nearer to 10
5  8 o'clock
6  Ninth
7  3 boxes
8  Shaded circle
9  5
10  6 socks

## Task 3d

## Task 4a
1   9
2   0
3   8
4   7
5   3
6   42
7   15 kg is more
8   7
9   6
10   5

## Task 4b
1   January
2   5 o'clock
3   3 sides
4   100 cm
5   13
6   17, 23, 32, 71
7   5 days
8   3
9   2p, 2p, 2p
10   White

## Task 4c
1   3
2   6
3   60
4   10
5   6
6   June
7   12
8   2
9   2
10   8

## Task 4d
1   6p
2   9p
3   A lollipop
4   8p
5   5p
6   2p
7   5 toffees
8   5p
9   5p and 2p
10   5p and 5p

## Task 5a
1   10
2   10
3   4
4   2
5   5
6   61 is more
7   9
8   100
9   4
10   9

## Task 5b
1   Half past 8
2   Centimetres
3   Wednesday
4   12 months
5   Three coins
6   432
7   0
8   7
9   36
10   A rectangle

## Task 5c

| 6 | 4 | 0 |
|---|---|---|
| 2 |   | 5 |
| 2 | 3 | 5 |

## Task 5d
1   4
2   9
3   12 is less
4   3
5   1
6   9
7   2p, 2p, 1p
8   0
9   5
10   12

## Task 6a
1   3 corners
2   4 months
3   Kilograms
4   5p, 2p, 1p
5   Half
6   14 conkers
7   1 hr (60 mins)
8   16p
9   4 days
10   6 apples

## Task 6b
1   10p
2   10
3   12
4   11
5   4
6   6 and 4
7   15p
8   12
9   10
10   73 is greater

## Task 6c
a.

| 4 | 2 | 5 | 1 |
|---|---|---|---|
| 3 | 1 | 2 | 2 |
| 3 | 3 | 4 | 2 |
| 1 | 3 | 0 | 4 |

b.

| 2 | 1 | 6 | 1 |
|---|---|---|---|
| 7 | 2 | 3 | 2 |
| 2 | 1 | 6 | 1 |
| 7 | 2 | 3 | 2 |

## Task 6d
1   6
2   12
3   14
4   4
5   3
6   11
7   9
8   3
9   16 is less
10   100

## Task 7a
1   12
2   Nearer to 10
3   24 hours
4   13
5   100
6   8
7   4 kg
8   9
9   2
10   20

## Task 7b
1   A hexagon
2   Saturday
3   3 coins
4   12
5   cm (or inches)
6   14
7   4p
8   14 books
9   5 months
10   5 triangles

## Task 7c
1   4 tens (or 40)
2   60
3   7
4   Nearer to 20
5   8
6   10
7   Sat. and Sun.
8   70
9   14
10   20

## Task 7d

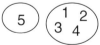

## Task 8a

1 Friday
2 18 children
3 4 corners
4 10p, 5p, 5p
5 Nearer 1 kg
6 2 halves
7 8 and 13
8 16
9 February
10 4, 1

## Task 8b

## Task 8c

1 8 o'clock
2 7p change
3 kg (or lbs)
4 12
5 15
6 19p
7 6 chews
8 5 pieces
9 12 hours
10 One half

## Task 8d

Tom has 19 books.

## Task 9a

1 **so** = 12
2 **do** = 6
3 **on** + **or** = 18
4 **ago** = 12
5 Yes: **odd** = 7
6 **sad** = 11
7 Both equal 11
8 **nor** – **add** = 8
9 **drag** = 10
10 **roars** = 19

## Task 9b

1 5
2 50
3 4
4 11
5 3
6 33
7 6
8 14
9 12
10 15

## Task 9c

1 3 hours
2 5 sides
3 About 7 cm
4 Nearer to 10
5 A rectangle
6 10p, 2p, 1p
7 77, 76, 70, 67
8 14 days
9 October
10 White

## Task 9d

1 90
2 11
3 20
4 8
5 9
6 12
7 16
8 19
9 9
10 9

## Task 10a

1 12
2 15
3 5
4 17
5 9
6 3
7 16
8 3
9 30
10 2

## Task 10b

| 1p | 3p | 2p |
|----|----|----|
| 3p | 2p | 1p |
| 2p | 1p | 3p |

or reflections
or rotations of this

## Task 10c

1 60
2 20
3 11
4 9
5 21
6 12
7 18
8 5
9 24
10 13

## Task 10d

1 Metres
2 11 o'clock
3 An octagon
4 January
5 2 boxes
6 9 marbles
7 5p, 2p, 2p, 1p
8 One quarter
9 Nearer 1 m
10 6 rectangles

## Task 11a

1 Half past four
2 Monday
3 6 sides
4 Autumn
5 38p
6 4 quarters
7 Metres (or ft)
8 A pentagon
9 10 eggs
10 5 people

## Task 11b

1 80
2 11
3 14
4 9
5 7
6 15
7 15
8 4
9 Ten 2p coins
10 18

## Task 11c

1 69
2 17
3 99
4 8
5 23
6 15
7 5
8 20
9 20
10 2

## Task 11d

| 1 | 4 | 7 | 6 |
|---|---|---|---|
| 9 |   |   | 10 |
| 8 | 3 | 5 | 2 |

| 9 | 0 | 7 | 3 |
|---|---|---|---|
| 8 |   |   | 5 |
| 2 | 3 | 3 | 11 |

| 2 | 3 | 5 | 10 |
|---|---|---|----|
| 17 |   |   | 6 |
| 1 | 13 | 2 | 4 |

Answers: *Mental Maths 1*

## Task 12a

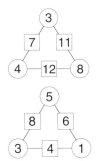

## Task 12b

1 Litres
2 7 and 9
3 07:30 (7:30 am)
4 November
5 8 corners
6 Three quarters
7 70
8 5p, 5p, 5p
9 Nearer 30 kg
10 Friday

## Task 12c

1 Winter
2 5 litres
3 A semi-circle
4 km or miles
5 4
6 102
7 4 ropes
8 Two 5p coins
9 6 birds
10 6 squares

## Task 12d

a.
$5-4+3+2-1=5$
or
$5+4-3-2+1=5$

b.
$2+2-3+4-5=0$

## Task 13a

1 8 catches
2 Peter
3 11 catches
4 14 catches
5 Peter
6 7 catches
7 12 catches
8 11 catches
9 Ann
10 8 more

## Task 13b

1 23
2 9 tens (or 90)
3 14
4 8
5 16
6 One half
7 20
8 40
9 18
10 10p, 5p, 2p, 2p

## Task 13c

1 1000 g in a kg
2 3:30 (or 03.30)
3 2 edges
4 2 weeks
5 One half
6 Spring
7 150
8 20 cm short
9 3
10 13

## Task 13d

1 90
2 – (minus)
3 5
4 80
5 15
6 6
7 14
8 34
9 28
10 1

## Task 14a

1 5
2 4
3 2p
4 6
5 45
6 + (plus)
7 16
8 13
9 48
10 4 coins

## Task 14b

1 12 marbles
2 12 gloves
3 3 packets
4 40
5 3 cakes each
6 10p
7 A circle
8 50 cm
9 20
10 20p

## Task 14c

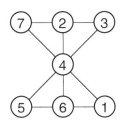

Other arrangements
are possible.

## Task 14d

1 14
2 0
3 4
4 54
5 101
6 × (times)
7 8
8 2
9 1
10 14

## Task 15a

1 11
2 January
3 The triangle
4 Summer
5 1000 ml in 1 l
6 About 20 kg
7 Two wholes
8 4 coins
9 Midnight
10 One quarter

## Task 15b

1 100
2 ÷ (divided by)
3 One whole
4 11
5 96
6 24 is even
7 30
8 89
9 3 and a half
10 110

## Task 15c

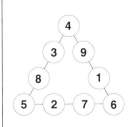

## Task 15d

1 One half
2 10
3 23
4 50
5 21 is odd
6 0
7 410
8 8
9 24
10 54

# Answers: *Mental maths 2*

*Mental Maths 2* reinforces the use of addition and subtraction facts to 20. It develops addition and subtraction of 10, then 100, to or from two- or three-digit numbers. The 2, 5 and 10 times tables are covered, and others in the range 1 to 25, with simple problems involving remainders. The tasks cover place value of numbers up to 1000, then beyond, rounding to the nearest 10 or 100, use of simple fractions and decimals (halves, quarters, fifths, tenths), telling the time (quarter to and quarter past), simple estimates with common metric measures, use of all coins, and recognising 3D shapes.

## Task 1a
1  55
2  16
3  26
4  £1
5  8
6  5
7  35
8  10
9  40
10  8

## Task 1b
1  8
2  3.5 kg
3  21
4  30 minutes
5  61, 60, 59
6  9 goals
7  10
8  20p, 5p, 2p
9  4p change
10  6 triangles

## Task 1c
1  24
2  10
3  9
4  31 days
5  25
6  A cube
7  0
8  50p, 10p
9  20
10  100

## Task 1d

| 4 | 3 | 3 |
|---|---|---|
| 1 |   | 5 |
| 5 | 3 | 2 |

## Task 2a
1  1 right angle
2  38p
3  5 minutes
4  16 tyres
5  14
6  7 people
7  £24
8  50
9  30 seconds
10  2 left turns

## Task 2b
1  9
2  18
3  17
4  3
5  5
6  20p, 20p, 10p
7  25
8  110
9  5p
10  14

## Task 2c
1  24
2  190
3  5
4  11
5  9
6  350
7  4
8  20p, 10p, 2p, 1p
9  365 (leap 366)
10  30

## Task 2d
Some solutions are:

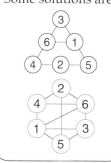

## Task 3a
1  8
2  66, 68, 86, 88
3  40 kg
4  409
5  17 cm
6  Ten 10p coins
7  16
8  £14
9  13, 27, 21
10  45 mins (3/4 h)

## Task 3b
E.g.

With 1 or 9 in the centre, lines with totals of 12 or 18 can be made.

## Task 3c
1  A cone
2  100 cm
3  70 years
4  3 packets
5  5
6  £1.10
7  1 litre
8  12
9  4 more
10  2 right angles

## Task 3d
1  7
2  17
3  20
4  25
5  30
6  30 days
7  280
8  12 legs
9  2 hours
10  50

## Task 4a

1   9
2   30
3   £5
4   20
5   23
6   9
7   5 and a half
8   4
9   9
10  106

## Task 4b

## Task 4c

1   £1.50
2   30
3   21
4   7
5   8 cm
6   24
7   31 days
8   12
9   2 kg
10  Nearer to 80

## Task 4d

1   C – A
2   A + E
3   B – A
4   B + D
5   D – B
6   E – C
7   C – B
8   B + C
9   D – A
10  A + C

## Task 5a

1   22
2   2
3   8
4   10
5   8
6   10p
7   35
8   28 days (29)
9   17
10  999

## Task 5b

1   200
2   80 litres
3   30 miles
4   6
5   A cylinder
6   No
7   800
8   10 children
9   Quarter past 3
10  A: 5p, 10p
    B: None

## Task 5c

1   12
2   23
3   40
4   50
5   9
6   3
7   36
8   106 is less
9   4
10  12 km

## Task 5d

Solutions must
have this pattern.

| E | O | E |
|---|---|---|
| O | O | O |
| E | O | E |

O=odd
E=even

One solution is:

| 2 | 5 | 6 |
|---|---|---|
| 9 | 3 | 1 |
| 4 | 7 | 8 |

## Task 6a

1   13 and 7
2   500
3   8 pairs
4   3 litres
5   80
6   12p
7   A pyramid
8   11
9   3.5 hours
10  72p

## Task 6b

1   5
2   7
3   53
4   5
5   26
6   40
7   48
8   1010
9   22 shoes
10  25

## Task 6c

| 6 | 1 | 8 |
|---|---|---|
| 7 | 5 | 3 |
| 2 | 9 | 4 |

15

| 10 | 2 | 9 |
|----|---|---|
| 6  | 7 | 8 |
| 5  | 12| 4 |

21

| 11 | 3 | 10 |
|----|---|----|
| 7  | 8 | 9  |
| 6  | 13| 5  |

24

## Task 6d

1   26
2   76
3   10
4   25
5   21
6   £15
7   1000 metres
8   20
9   20
10  400

## Task 7a

1   8
2   10
3   33
4   21
5   11
6   45
7   8 coins
8   103
9   42
10  1029

## Task 7b

1   111, 110, 101, 100
2   Even
3   110 km/h
4   60
5   10, 15, 40
6   £1.50
7   20 horse-shoes
8   10 litres
9   10
10  14th February

## Task 7c

1   6
2   10
3   66
4   100
5   30
6   41
7   798
8   26th December
9   26
10  13

## Task 7d

1   a. Friday
    b. Saturday
    c. Sunday
    d. Saturday
    e. Monday (leap)
2   a. 6th November
    b. 3rd November
    c. 28th November
    d. 19th November
    e. 5th November

## Task 8a

| Island | Mainland |
|---|---|
| 8:15 a.m. | 9:00 a.m. |
| 10:15 a.m. | 9:30 a.m. |
| 10:45 a.m. | 11:30 a.m. |
| 12:45 p.m. | 12 noon |
| 1:15 p.m. | 2:00 p.m. |
| 3:15 p.m. | 2:30 p.m. |

## Task 8b

3 4    1 2 5 6

2 5    1 4 3 6

1 6    2 3 5 4

1 2 4    3 6 5

## Task 8c

1. 25 cm
2. West
3. One fifth
4. 35p
5. A stamp
6. 95 cm
7. 6 goals
8. Quarter to 4
9. About 10 m
10. 2 sweets

## Task 8d

1. 7
2. Odd
3. 24
4. 12
5. 35
6. 100
7. 18
8. 104
9. 40
10. 1000 g

## Task 9a

8  1  22  5
1
14  9  3  5
4  1  25

HAVE
A
NICE
DAY

## Task 9b

a.
$5+3-1+3-5=5$
or
$5-3+1-3+5=5$

b.
$12-3+4-5+6=14$

## Task 9c

1. 10 rectangles
2. −5
3. 20 coins
4. 763
5. 6 hours
6. 500 ml
7. 7
8. 5 tickets
9. 8 cm
10. 26p

## Task 9d

1. 27
2. 6
3. 21
4. 38
5. 8
6. 20
7. 177
8. 40
9. 67
10. 350

## Task 10a

1. 64
2. 12
3. 23
4. 44
5. 491
6. 6
7. −1
8. 390
9. 33
10. 50p, 20p, 5p, 1p

## Task 10b

1. 30 chicks
2. 2
3. 180°
4. 15
5. 76 and 56
6. 1 hr (or adjust)
7. Three quarters
8. A triangle
9. £1.10
10. 23°C

## Task 10c

1. 15
2. 8
3. 157
4. 6
5. 23
6. 24
7. 475
8. 50p, 20p, 20p
9. 33
10. 1000

## Task 10d

a.

| 4 | 3 | 5 | 6 |
|---|---|---|---|
| 4 | 4 | 3 | 1 |
| 7 | 0 | 8 | 3 |
| 1 | 7 | 0 | 4 |

b.

| 6 | 4 | 7 | 1 |
|---|---|---|---|
| 5 | 5 | 4 | 8 |
| 2 | 8 | 3 | 5 |
| 3 | 7 | 2 | 10 |

## Task 11a

1. 5 children
2. 25p
3. A circle
4. 6 scones each
5. 600
6. 50p, 20p, 2p
7. 250 g
8. 4 left over
9. 7 rows
10. 40 seconds

## Task 11b

1. 5
2. 12
3. 21
4. 31
5. 45
6. 370
7. 357
8. 5 coins
9. 7
10. 3

## Task 11c

1. 22
2. 0
3. 47
4. 246
5. 92
6. 15 minutes
7. 21
8. A cylinder
9. 35
10. £1.09 is less

## Task 11d

[1 1]  [1 6]  [6 5]
[2 2]  [2 4]  [4 6]
[2 2]  [2 5]  [5 4]*
[3 3]  [3 5]  [5 1]
[4 4]  [4 1]  [1 6]
[4 4]  [4 3]  [3 2]
[5 5]  [5 1]  [1 3]
[5 5]  [5 2]  [2 1]

*Shown in example

## Task 12a

1   90°
2   150 g
3   £1.60
4   4 left over
5   345
6   40
7   10p
8   15
9   18
10  Three fifths

## Task 12b

| 1 | 2 | 4 | 8 |
| 5 | ✗ | 2 | 3 |
| 7 | 7 | 1 | ⊗ |
| 2 | 6 | 3 | 9 |

## Task 12c

1   55
2   6
3   25
4   60
5   227
6   11
7   410
8   A sphere
9   £2.67
10  9

## Task 12d

1   A circle
2   £4.30
3   6 packets
4   Seven 5s
5   £3.60
6   –5 °C
7   £60
8   2101
9   4 people
10  8 triangles

## Task 13a

1   10:30 a.m.
2   1 hr 30 mins
3   45 people
4   After midday
5   10 people
6   5 people
7   30 empty seats
8   £5
9   60
10  200 seats

## Task 13b

6 houses in Lime
Street.

## Task 13c

1   £3
2   45 seconds
3   5 litres
4   400
5   2
6   6 ribbons
7   5 faces
8   80
9   2p left over
10  50p, 5p, 2p

## Task 13d

1   30
2   18
3   12
4   3
5   30
6   Nearer 100
7   62
8   15
9   16
10  8

## Task 14a

1   28
2   20
3   470
4   12
5   63
6   × (times)
7   45 seconds
8   0.5
9   25 coins
10  900

## Task 14b

1   £4.50
2   110 sweets
3   White
4   20
5   4 °C
6   5 coins
7   5005
8   £11.05
9   £3.60
10  14 squares

## Task 14c

Other solutions are
possible.

| 1p | 4p | 3p | 2p |
| 2p | 3p | 4p | 1p |
| 4p | 1p | 2p | 3p |
| 3p | 2p | 1p | 4p |

## Task 14d

1   27
2   10
3   15
4   145 cm
5   246
6   50p, 50p, 1p
7   980
8   + (plus)
9   6 faces
10  0.25

## Task 15a

1   30
2   2
3   22
4   2.26 metres
5   338
6   A cuboid
7   80
8   50p, 20p, 5p, 2p
9   0.9
10  200

## Task 15b

1   501, 500, 499
2   9 cakes
3   18th
4   8 hours
5   21
6   50p, 80p
7   £6.04
8   140 kg
9   9 choc-drops
10  6 baskets

## Task 15c

1   Even
2   25
3   140 cm
4   38
3   3169
6   12 edges
7   32
8   70
9   No
10  10

## Task 15d

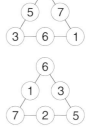